MAGNIFYING YOUR
AARONIC
PRIESTHOOD
CALLING

MAGNIFYING YOUR
AARONIC
PRIESTHOOD
CALLING

SHANE R. BARKER

Bookcraft
Salt Lake City, Utah

Library of Congress Catalog Card Number: 95-75087
ISBN 0-88494-977-X

First Printing, 1995

Printed in the United States of America

For Bryan, Ben, and Aaron

CONTENTS

Contents

CRASHING ON AN INNER TUBE!

Chapter One

Magnifying Your Aaronic Priesthood Calling

"This is nuts!"

Marissa Kay shivered as she wrapped her arms around me. "I mean, it's *crazy!* I can't believe we're really doing this."

"Oh, come on," I said as I gripped the sides of the inner tube. "It only looks scary."

"Right," Marissa replied, tightening her grip. "And it'll only hurt when we hit the bottom."

I laughed. "Are you ready?"

"Yes, I'm ready."

I looked up at my friend Tyson and nodded. "Okay, push us off."

"All right," Tyson said. "On the count of three. One . . . two . . . three!" He shoved, pushing us onto the icy slope. An instant later we were flying over the snow like a pair of luge racers going for the gold. The night wind stung my face and burned my lungs as we zoomed down the hillside. Marissa was screaming in my ear, "Shaaaaaaane!"

We hit a bump and flew through the air, then smacked hard onto the snow. We bounced and spun down the hill out of control, finally plowing into a bank of soft snow.

Marissa was laughing so hard that I had to help her to her feet.

"That was so fun!" she said. "Let's do it again!"

"All right!" I grabbed the tube and followed her back up the hill.

It was Christmas vacation, and I was tubing with friends from my BYU student ward. Looking back, we should have known we were asking for trouble. It was night, for one thing, and we had nothing but the light of the stars to see by.

But the worst thing was that we'd picked the steepest hill on the mountain to tube on. It dropped off like a roller coaster and had so many bumps that we felt like we were tubing down a flight of stairs.

But I had to admit, we were having fun!

When we reached the top of the hill, Tyson was standing in the takeoff area with his girlfriend, Laura.

"Was it scary?" Laura asked.

"Naw," I lied. "It's great. You'll love it."

"I bet," Laura said.

I held the tube as Tyson piled aboard and Laura gingerly crawled on after him.

"Hold on tight," I warned them.

"Don't worry," Laura said. "I'm not letting go for anything."

"Okay, then," I said. "On the count of three. One . . . two . . ." Without waiting for *three* I pushed, sliding them onto the slope.

Tyson and Laura both screamed at once.

"Aaaaaaiiiiigggggghhhhh!"

They flew down the hill, screaming in the wind as they zoomed over the snow and picked up speed. They were shooting straight for the bottom and were almost in the clear when, without warning, they hit a bump, flew through the air, and wiped out. The tube went right, Tyson went left, and Laura snowballed down the hill into a tree.

"Laura!"

Dropping our tubes, we raced down the hill, everyone expecting the worst. By the time we reached the bottom, Tyson was up and rubbing his head—but Laura wasn't moving.

"Don't move her!" Marissa warned. "If she's hurt, you could make things worse."

I pulled off my coat and draped it over Laura's still form as Marissa softly patted her cheeks.

"Laura? Laura, can you hear me?"

No answer.

We all looked at one another, all of us worried sick. For all we knew, Laura had a concussion. Or a broken neck. Or both. As we stood in the snow, wondering what to do, Marissa spoke up. "You guys have to give her a blessing."

I'm ashamed to admit it, but that was one of the worst moments of my life. The thought of using the priesthood to give Laura a blessing scared me. There were certain things in my life that weren't in order, things I needed to repent of, and I wasn't worthy to administer a priesthood blessing.

I felt terrible. One of my friends was hurt and needed a blessing, and I wasn't worthy to give her one.

Fortunately, my friends Tyson and James *were* worthy. They gave Laura a blessing, and a few minutes later she moaned, blinked, and opened her eyes. She had a black eye and a fat lip for a week, but other than that she wasn't hurt.

But I learned a powerful lesson. I learned that you never know when you're going to need the power of the priesthood. You never know when the Lord is going to call on you or when you will need to call on him.

You have to be ready all the time.

I was exploring a cave once with a couple of my friends. We spent hours crawling through the rocks and the dust, and when it came time to leave we couldn't find the way out.

Talk about scary! We were so mixed up and turned around that we had no idea which way to even *start* looking for a way out. To conserve batteries, we turned off all of our flashlights but one, then sat down and tried to decide what to do.

My friend Mark suggested that we say a prayer. Most of us had been praying frantically for several minutes anyway, but we decided that a group prayer would be a good idea too.

Someone asked Mark to offer the prayer and he agreed. We all knelt in the dust, took off our rock helmets, and bowed our heads.

Right away, I was glad we had chosen Mark to be our spokesman. He prayed with the calm, quiet confidence of a young man who was close to his Father in Heaven and who knew his prayer would be answered.

The effect was magical. Minutes earlier we were all scared, worried, and frightened. But suddenly we were calm, quiet, and confident. And fifteen minutes later, we found our way out.

I've never forgotten those experiences. They've reminded me that you can't fool the Lord. You can pretend to be worthy of your priesthood, but when the chips are down and you need the power of the Lord behind you, you can't pretend anymore.

Now you hold the Aaronic Priesthood. As you grow older, you'll have many opportunities to use it. When you do, like I was you might be hesitant, afraid, or unworthy to act in the name of your Father in Heaven.

But if you keep yourself worthy and if you *magnify* your priesthood calling, you'll be able to do your work with confidence. Like Mark, you'll be able to approach your Heavenly Father knowing that he approves of what you're doing and that he will answer your prayers.

Remember that priesthood service isn't something you are automatically good at. Like an athlete, you have to practice, exercise, and work at it. Then, in time, you get better, stronger, and more confident. The more you use the priesthood, the more it will bless your life and the more powerful it will be when you need it.

Besides, magnifying your priesthood calling is something the Lord expects you to do.

Remember the parable of the talents? Jesus told of a man who gave each of his servants certain talents. Later, the man spoke with his servants to see what they'd done with their gifts. Those who had increased their talents were blessed and given more. The one who had done nothing was cursed, and his talent was taken away.

You see, it's not enough to simply *have* the priesthood. You must make the most of it. By doing so, you prepare yourself for additional gifts from God. You prepare yourself for greater responsibilities. Your experiences as a deacon, teacher, and priest, for example, prepare you for service in the Melchizedek Priesthood. They prepare you for your mission. They prepare you for leadership in wards and stakes.

Who knows? They might even be preparing you to preside over the Church.

That's why it's important to magnify each priesthood calling you receive. Whether you're a newly ordained deacon, an elder about to serve a mission, or the most senior of the Twelve Apostles, you are capable of growing. No matter what office you hold, you can accept your calling and magnify it.

That's what this book is all about. It's about learning to magnify your priesthood calling. It's about taking the power and authority the Lord has given you and learning to use it to serve others. You'll find the priesthood expanding your abilities, increasing your spiritual and physical strength, and making you more powerful.

Start now! Whether you're a deacon, a teacher, or a priest, decide to make the priesthood you bear an important part of your life. Decide to magnify your calling to the best of your ability. As you do, you'll become closer to your Heavenly Father. You will create for yourself a shield from evil. Your spirit will grow strong, and you'll receive blessings not only in this life but throughout all eternity.

"LOOK!
IT'S SHERLOCK HOLMES!"

Chapter Two

What It Means to Magnify Your Priesthood Calling

Brother Warner crept into quorum meeting holding a magnifying glass. He was wearing a deerstalker cap and sneaking about like Sherlock Holmes on an important case.

"Shhhh," he whispered, holding a finger to his lips. "I'm looking for clues."

He tiptoed around the room, peering at things through his magnifying glass, once in a while embarrassing someone by examining his ears or peering into his mouth. Everyone grinned, anxious to find out what he was up to.

Next to my dad, Brother Warner was the most incredible man I ever knew. He was my deacons quorum adviser, and everyone enjoyed his lessons because they were so much fun. His stories would have everyone in the room crying one minute, then howling with laughter the next. He was always doing something outrageous to make a point.

Like now. He continued his investigation for another couple of minutes, then surprised everyone by holding his magnifying glass up to his eye.

"Wow!" he said. "Everything seems so big when I look through this."

"Well, *duh*," someone said. "It's a *magnifying* glass."

"A magnifying glass? What does that mean?"

My friend Cannon struggled for an answer. "It makes things bigger."

Brother Warner pretended to be confused. "Makes things bigger? Then what does it mean to magnify your priesthood calling?"

"To make it grow?"

Brother Warned jumped forward, startling everyone. "Yes! That's it! You magnify your priesthood calling by making it grow!" He looked each one of us in the eyes. "Now, will you do that? Will you magnify your priesthood?"

"Yes!" we chorused.

I was so excited that I rushed home right after church, anxious to get started. There was only one problem.

I didn't know what to do.

I had heard about "magnifying my priesthood calling" before. It sounded like a good thing to do. But when it came right down to it, I had no idea what it meant. It was several years, in fact, before I finally understood what it meant to magnify a priesthood calling.

Let me give you an example.

When I was sixteen, I had a friend named Chris who was called to be first assistant to the bishop in his priests quorum. From the very first day he was determined to do the best job he could. He did, too. He attacked his duties with the energy of a hurricane. Under the direction of the bishop, he organized firesides with the Laurels. He invited returned missionaries to get the quorum fired up about missionary work. He visited the teachers and deacons quorums to help them understand the sacred nature of the sacrament.

But that wasn't all. He set an example by volunteering for assignments. He did his home teaching. He stayed close to everyone in the quorum, helping them to stay strong and active in the Church.

You see, Chris knew what it took to be a great leader. He did more than sit in the back of the room yawning, scratching, and doodling in his notebook. He took an active part. He worked. He studied. He went the extra mile to serve his quorum as well as he could.

That's how Chris magnified his priesthood calling, and that's how you can magnify yours. Take the power and responsibilities the Lord has given you and do your best with them. Your *very best*.

Sound tough?

It's not! In fact, when you magnify your priesthood calling, you invite the Spirit of the Lord to be with you. You invite the constant companionship of the Holy Ghost, and many of the things you need to do will become almost automatic.

Are you still wondering what to do? Here are a few ideas:

Be Willing to Serve

One of the first—and best—ways you can magnify your priesthood calling is by serving your Father in Heaven and his children every way you can. Volunteer for assignments such as visiting rest homes, working on the welfare farm, saying prayers in meetings, and giving talks or lessons.

Lots of people do things when they're asked. But go the extra mile: don't wait to be asked. When your adviser or a member of your quorum presidency needs a volunteer, be the first one in the room with your hand up. Show your Heavenly Father through your actions that he can count on you when there's a job to be done.

Keep Yourself Worthy of Holding the Priesthood

When you prepare, bless, or pass the sacrament, your hands should be clean. Just as important, your heart should be clean too.

As you grow older, the temptations you face will become stronger and more powerful. There may be times when resisting them will make you feel like David standing up to Goliath.

When that happens, remember that David won his battle. You can beat your Goliaths too. Just as David used a slingshot and stones—weapons he was familiar with through much use—you can use weapons such as scriptures, prayer, fasting, and blessings to overcome the special challenges of your life.

Make it a special point to obey the Word of Wisdom (remember that this includes such things as exercising, eating right, and taking care of yourself, as well as not smoking or drinking). Keep yourself free from immoral practices. And be sure that your speech is appropriate for someone who holds the priesthood: never swear or use vulgar or suggestive expressions.

Finally, stay close to your bishop. When you face difficult challenges, share them with him. Seek his help and guidance. Let him help you to keep your life clean and pure.

Dress Modestly

There are not many things that young people resent more than having adults telling them how to dress. But when you were baptized, you took upon yourself the name of Jesus Christ. When you were ordained to the priesthood, you became his representative. You should reflect this, both in the way you act and the way you dress.

When you participate in priesthood ordinances, such as administering the sacrament or assisting with ordinations, dress in a way that will invite the Spirit of the Lord. Wear nice, clean clothes, including a white shirt and a tie if possible.

Remember that what you wear is not as important as why you wear it. When you represent your Savior, your clothing shouldn't be chosen to display your school spirit or taste in fashions. It should signify your respect for your Father in Heaven.

Keep in mind that you represent your Savior when you're away from church too. People see you every day at work and school, and many of them follow your example. Be sure that your influence is good, both in the way you act and the way you dress.

This doesn't mean that you need to wear white shirts and ties all the time. But don't wear clothes that are immodest or that advertise alcohol, tobacco, or other things the Lord would disapprove of.

Learn About the Priesthood

You can't truly begin to magnify your priesthood calling until you know what the priesthood is. So find out! Learn what you can do with it. Discover what the Lord expects of you in your priesthood calling, and learn what blessings you'll receive in return.

Start by reading sections 20, 84, and 107 of the Doctrine and Covenants. Then trace your priesthood lineage. Start with the person who ordained you. Find out who gave him the authority to do that, and then where that person got his authority, and so on. See if you can trace your authority back to Peter, James, and John, and then to Jesus Christ.

I was ordained a teacher, for instance, by my dad, who was ordained an elder by my grandfather. My grandfather was ordained a high priest by Adam S. Bennion.

Adam S. Bennion was ordained an Apostle by David O. McKay.

David O. McKay was ordained an Apostle by Joseph F. Smith.

Joseph F. Smith was ordained an Apostle by Brigham Young.

Brigham Young was ordained an Apostle by Oliver Cowdery, David Whitmer, and Martin Harris, who were ordained by Joseph Smith, Sidney Rigdon, and Frederick G. Williams.

Joseph Smith and Oliver Cowdery received the Melchizedek Priesthood from Peter, James, and John.

Peter, James, and John were ordained Apostles by Jesus Christ.

The Church of Jesus Christ of Latter-day Saints is the only church in which priesthood leaders can trace their authority directly to Jesus Christ. Trace yours as proof that you have the authority to represent Jesus Christ and to act in his name.

Strive to Improve Yourself

In the first chapter we talked about the parable of the talents. Jesus made it clear that he expects you to make the most of whatever gifts he has given you. This applies to all gifts, not just spiritual ones.

If you have a knack for music, for example, take advantage of it. Play in the school band. Share your talent in concerts and festivals. Take private lessons to become better, if you can.

We live in troubled times, and the Lord needs young men with momentum on his side. He needs young men who are better than average, young men who are better than mediocre.

This means that you need to follow the Scout Oath, doing your best in school, sports, art, or whatever it is that you choose to do.

A good way to start is by picking out two or three things that are important in your life, things like school, music, or sports. Pinpoint ways that you can do better in those areas, and then follow through. Make the most of whatever gifts and talents the Lord has given you.

By quietly, consistently striving to improve yourself, your example will shine out to those around you. You'll motivate and influence others, and you'll magnify your priesthood calling.

Pray Often

One sure way to become close to your Heavenly Father is to pray often. But your prayers must be meaningful.

When I was earning my pilot's license, I was once flying from Ogden to Provo when a red light began flashing on my instrument panel. Being a student pilot, I didn't know how much danger I was in, so I began to pray. I mean, I really began to pray! I prayed as if my life depended on it, because at the time I thought it did!

Later I wondered what my life would be like if every prayer I said was as sincere and heartfelt as that one.

When you pray, don't simply pray out of habit, just to get it over with. Instead, talk with your Father in Heaven.

Discuss your needs and problems with him, sharing your feelings, concerns, doubts, and worries. Try to picture him in your mind, and pray like you know he's listening.

Then remain on your knees for a moment and reflect on the things you've prayed about. Be sensitive for answers.

If you pray often, consistently offering sincere, meaningful prayers, you'll grow closer to your Heavenly Father. You'll find it easier to resist temptation and to do the things required to magnify your priesthood calling.

As you learn about and serve in your Aaronic Priesthood office and calling, the priesthood will become a powerful force in your life. You'll become closer to your Father in Heaven and enjoy the constant companionship of the Holy Ghost. The priesthood will help prepare you for your mission, college, and adult life, blessing you in ways you never knew possible.

So be proud that you hold the priesthood. Get excited about it! Serve wherever and whenever you can. Keep yourself worthy. Dress modestly and learn as much you can. Finally, remember to pray often.

As you do, your life will change, and the Lord will bless your home and family as you never thought possible. And priesthood service will become a source of never-ending happiness.

KNOTS, LASHINGS, AND PEPPERONI PIZZA

Chapter Three

Strengthening Your Quorum

Justin Smith charged across the park with a frantic look in his eye. "Quick!" he shouted. "I need somebody to splice some ropes!"

Treavor Marshall looked up from the pile of poles he was sorting and raised his hand. "I'll do it!"

"Hurry!" Justin shouted. "We need you over here!"

Treavor didn't wait to be asked twice. He ran off with Justin and began splicing like his life depended on it.

I grinned.

It was Saturday morning, and the Scout troop I worked with was competing in the district Scout-o-Rama. Our troop was assigned to build a tower, which didn't happen to be a major chore. But just before we got started, our Scoutmaster, Brother Miller, decided to make things complicated.

"Troop 747 is building a tower on the other side of the

park," he told us. "And they think theirs is going to be better than ours."

The troop responded with boos and catcalls.

Brother Miller smiled. "I thought you'd feel that way," he said. "So I challenged them to a contest."

Justin, our senior patrol leader, spoke up: "What kind of contest?"

Brother Miller shrugged as if it wasn't any big deal. "Well, it's more of a race, really. I told them we could build our tower faster and better than they could build theirs. And"—he paused for a second—"I told them we'd buy them a pizza if we couldn't."

"What if *we* win?" Justin asked. "Do they have to buy *us* pizza?"

"Yes."

The troop responded with enthusiasm.

"All right, then!"

"Let's do it!"

"Yeah! Let's get started!"

The Scouts tore into their work like gangbusters. They lashed poles, pounded stakes, and tied knots with the energy of teenage tornadoes. Justin, knowing that Brother Miller was a stickler for accuracy, paced around with a *Scout Handbook*, double-checking knots and lashings, making certain everything was perfect.

About the time the tower was half finished, the Scoutmaster of the rival troop wandered over.

"Hi," he said to Brother Miller, loud enough for everyone to hear. "Strange thing . . . I just left my troop, and everyone's talking about having pizza for lunch today."

The Scouts began working even faster.

Across the park, Troop 747 was working just as hard. Scouts whooped and shouted as they lashed their poles and tied their knots.

As far as I could tell, the towers were going up with equal speed. Everyone knew the race was going to be close, so as soon as the last knot was tied, Justin grabbed Brother Miller and dragged him over.

"Quick!" he shouted. "Inspect it!"

Brother Miller stroked his chin. "Hmmmm," he said, leisurely glancing up at the tower. "It seems to be sturdy enough. But maybe I should inspect these knots. . . ."

Justin looked across the park. Scouts from the rival troop had their tower up and were pleading for permission to climb it.

There wasn't any more time.

"Come on!" he shouted. "We're taking Brother Miller hostage!"

With that, the Scouts scrambled up the tower, taking Brother Miller with them.

The Scoutmasters decided to call the contest a tie, but since everyone got pizza no one seemed to mind. We ate ours on top of the tower.

"I want you to think about something," Brother Miller said as he wiped a spot of cheese from his chin. "You boys worked together to build this tower. It took all of you to do it. But now that it's up, *it's* supporting *you*."

He took a moment to make sure everyone was listening before he continued. "Now, I want you to understand that our deacons quorum is just like that. It takes all of us to make our quorum. But why do you suppose that's important? Why do you suppose we have a quorum?"

Treavor shrugged. "To support us?"

"That's right!" Brother Miller pointed at each Scout in turn. "The purpose of our quorum is to support you. To serve you. And you. And you."

The boys were all looking at the tower with new understanding. I was too. I was an elder at the time, but I suddenly

17

understood the purpose of quorums in a way that I never had before.

You see, as soon as you receive the Aaronic Priesthood, you join a quorum. As you grow older, you change quorums from time to time, but you're always part of a quorum somewhere.

And that's great! No matter where you go, no matter how old you are, you always have a quorum watching you, looking out for you, standing by to help you when you need it.

I know a young man named Ben who became inactive in the Church. He quit attending meetings. He quit going to activities. He decided that he wasn't going to serve a mission.

But even though Ben lost interest in his quorum, his quorum didn't lose interest in him. No one in the quorum was especially close to Ben, but everyone liked him. They realized that he was too important to let drift away, so they began working on him. Whenever the quorum had an activity, someone invited Ben. Whenever there was a dance, someone called. Whenever there was a fireside, someone made sure Ben knew about it.

At first, Ben didn't respond. But one day the doorbell rang, and when he opened the door a boy named Deven was standing there.

"Hey," Deven said. "We're going to a dance. Wanna come?"

Ben nodded. "Sure."

A week or so later, Deven was back. "We're going over to Janna Ford's house for ice cream," he said. "Wanna come?"

Ben nodded again. "Sure."

Little by little, Deven and Ben became better friends. They spent more and more time together, and they gradually began showing up to quorum activities together. Pretty soon, Ben was going to church again. He was going to firesides. He began taking missionary prep classes.

Before long Ben was called to be second assistant in the priests quorum. He became an elder and served a mission.

"Going on a mission is the best thing I ever did," Ben told me. "I can't imagine what I'd be like if I hadn't gone, and it scares me to think what might have happened if the guys had given up on me."

Now, that's what your priesthood quorum is for—to watch out for you! To keep you doing what's right. To give you opportunities to serve, teach lessons, and build relationships, both with your priesthood brothers and with the young women in the ward.

And—by giving you opportunities to serve in a presidency—it can give you experience in leadership, conducting meetings, and delegating responsibility.

Belonging to a quorum is one of the greatest blessings you can ever receive as a young man.

Now, maybe your quorum is like that. And maybe it's not. If not, you can help make it that way. Like Deven, you can help fellowship less-active members. You can watch over your quorum brothers, giving them a hand when they need it, giving them a boost when they're down, giving them a pat on the back to keep them going.

Here are other ways to make your quorum successful:

Participate in Quorum Meetings

When you're in a quorum meeting, don't just sit in the corner and doodle—get involved with the lesson. Ask questions. Offer thoughts and ideas. Share inspirational experiences.

Your adviser might be the most awesome teacher in the

world. But no one knows what it's like to be a teenager better than a teenager, and your thoughts, experiences, and insights might be just what someone else needs to hear.

So if the lesson is on prayer and you've had an inspirational experience, share it! You'll make the meeting more interesting, and chances are that your experience will inspire someone else.

Keep in mind that quorum meeting is more than a class. It's an opportunity to build unity. It's a chance to develop brotherhood. But for those things to happen, you have to participate.

Participate in Quorum Activities

Not every activity your quorum plans is going to be your idea of fun. But go anyway! Remember that a trip to the ice rink is more than a chance to work on your skating—it's an opportunity to build quorum unity and brotherhood.

So go! The simple fact that you're there will make the activity more fun for others. Your influence, example, and friendship will bless and strengthen your brethren.

Besides, you never know when a member of your quorum might secretly be struggling. Something you do or say might be the key to getting him back on the right track again. It might give him the strength to hang on. The power of your friendship and companionship might be just the boost he needs to recharge his testimony and stay active in the Church.

Support Your Adviser

When I was a deacon, I was sitting on the front row waiting to pass the sacrament one Sunday when the bishop made a startling announcement.

"We'd like to release Brother Warner as our deacons quorum adviser."

The entire quorum sat in shock. Brother Warner was the most awesome adviser in the world! And he was a terrific Scoutmaster! As the members of the ward raised their hands, thanking him for his work, we began whispering back and forth.

"How can they do this to us?"

"They *can't* release Brother Warner!"

"We've got to talk to the bishop!"

"Yeah! We'll tell him that if he releases Brother Warner, we'll quit coming to church!"

As we sat conspiring to save our beloved leader, the bishop made another startling announcement.

"We'd now like to present for your sustaining vote Brother Jay Barker as deacons quorum adviser and Scoutmaster."

The quorum was suddenly silent again. "Brother Barker" was my dad.

My dad!

Suddenly we were full of excitement. My dad was Mr. Outdoors. He often went with us on trips and campouts, and everybody loved him. Our bishop had picked one of the few men in the ward we loved as much as Brother Warner.

And Dad didn't disappoint us. He took us on the most incredible campouts. He kept us busy, enthused, and excited. He was one of the best leaders I ever had.

Now, you probably have wonderful advisers too. If so, make sure they know how much you appreciate them. It takes a lot of work and energy to advise a quorum of teenage boys, and the more you support and sustain them, the better they'll be able to help you.

There may be times when you and your adviser don't

see eye to eye. At times like these, go out of your way to support him anyway. Remember that the Lord called him to work with you. Your Heavenly Father wants him working with you. No matter what the problem is, be sure you do whatever you can to work things out peacefully. Keep in mind that even when things don't turn out exactly the way you want them to, the Lord will bless you for trying.

Help Everyone to Feel Part of the Quorum

There's nothing worse than belonging to a group that you don't feel part of. One way for you to magnify your priesthood calling is to help every member of your quorum feel important, wanted, and needed.

If one of the guys is shy or lonely, go the extra mile to be his friend. Sit by him in meetings. Talk with him. Go with him to activities.

And if there's someone in your quorum who's always getting picked on, stand up for him. Be one person he knows he can always feel safe, happy, and comfortable with.

There's nothing your Heavenly Father will appreciate more than seeing you try to make everyone in the quorum feel welcome, wanted, and included.

Support Your Quorum Presidency

If you are ever called to serve in the presidency of your quorum, one of the first things you'll learn is that it's impossible to succeed without the support of everyone else.

Give your presidency the same support you would like to have yourself. Respect them by paying attention when they conduct quorum meetings. Cheerfully accept the assignments they give you. (More than that, make their job easier by volunteering for assignments when they come up.)

Then be enthusiastic. When your quorum leaders announce plans for an activity, show your excitement. Help spread enthusiasm among the rest of the quorum. Do everything you can to make the activity successful.

Keep in mind that the Lord called your presidency to lead your quorum. By supporting them, not only are you following your Heavenly Father, but you're magnifying your priesthood calling too.

Remember that the purpose of your quorum is to serve you. It's designed to teach you the gospel, strengthen your testimony, and prepare you for your mission. But you have responsibilities to your quorum too. When you actively strive to strengthen your quorum, the Lord will notice. He will bless you for your efforts.

So participate in your quorum meetings. Do your best to make every activity successful. Go out of your way to make everyone feel included. Support your quorum presidency and advisers, doing whatever you can to make their jobs easier.

Not only will you make your quorum better, stronger, and more effective, but you'll magnify your priesthood calling and help others magnify theirs.

"SOMEONE FORGOT TO STIR THE CHILI!"

Chapter Four

Magnifying Your Priesthood Calling as a Deacon

"Ick! Someone forgot to stir the chili!"

Mark Goff lifted a greasy pot from the wash water and pulled a face. "It's all burned to the bottom of the pot."

"Yuck," I said, peering into the pot and frowning at the gooey mess. "It must have been Scottie, the only guy in the troop who has trouble boiling water."

Mark grinned as he began scraping away the goo. "Scottie? Aren't you forgetting Jeff?"

I laughed, suddenly remembering the one Scout in the troop who cooked worse than Scottie. This was our third night at Scout camp, and the night before, Jeff—the youngest Scout in the troop—had cooked dinner. He'd heard that putting dish soap on the pots would make them easier to clean. What he didn't realize was that he was only supposed to soap the *outside* of the pot. His chicken gumbo not only tasted like soap but also gave everyone a little intestinal surprise.

Mark's grin widened. "You have to admit, though, those pots *were* easy to clean."

I stopped working and looked up. "That's right. You were on cleanup last night. Why are you doing it again?"

"Jason had a class, so I said I'd take his turn for him."

"Really? What do you get out of the deal?"

"Nothing. I just volunteered."

I smiled. It didn't surprise me that Mark was doing something like that. That's just the sort of boy Mark was.

I thought of one night several months earlier, when I had been driving home in the middle of a snowstorm. The storm was so bad that I had to put my truck in four-wheel drive to get through it. Cars were stuck in drifts all over town, and many people couldn't even get in or out of their own driveways. I wouldn't even have been out except that I had been to my mother's house, shoveling her walks.

Anyway, as I plowed through the snow, I spotted someone walking down the middle of the road. He was carrying a sleeping bag, and as I drove closer I realized it was Mark.

I pulled over and rolled down the window.

"Hey, Mark . . . is that you?"

He nodded, hunching his shoulders against the storm. "Yeah."

"You want a ride?"

He nodded eagerly. "Sure!"

He quickly climbed inside, tossing his sleeping bag behind the seat. "Thanks," he said, brushing the snow off his shoulders. "I can't believe how hard it's snowing!"

"I know," I said as I pulled back onto the road. "Where've you been?"

"At Brandon's. We were supposed to have a sleep-over."

"So how come you're going home? Something happen?"

He shrugged. "Well, his parents aren't home, and everybody's watching a movie that's kind of dirty." He shrugged again. "I just didn't like what was going on."

And so he was walking home. After dark. In the middle of a blizzard.

I admired Mark for that. He had shown a lot of courage to leave his friends in the middle of a party.

But then, that's the sort of boy Mark was.

When you think of being a deacon, you probably think about things like passing the sacrament and collecting fast offerings. Those are important duties. But there's more to it than that. When you accept the priesthood, you covenant to live the principles of the gospel. You promise to obey your Heavenly Father's commandments.

That's what Mark did. And that's what you should do too. Live your life in a way that you know your Heavenly Father would be pleased with. How do you do that? Easy! Whenever you find yourself in a situation where you're not sure what to do, just ask yourself, "What would Jesus do?" Then act accordingly.

I know that sounds corny. But if you do that, and if you honestly try to make decisions as you believe the Savior would, you'll never go wrong.

Being a deacon is a wonderful thing. You have more energy and enthusiasm during the ages of twelve and thirteen than almost any other time in your life. Your whole life is wide open and waiting for you. You have more opportunities to prepare for the future than you'll ever have again.

There's no finer time to be alive!

At the same time, being a deacon is a tremendous responsibility. You have great duties to perform. So let's look at ways you can magnify your priesthood calling as a deacon.

Passing the Sacrament

In the early days of the restored Church, deacons didn't always pass the sacrament. It wasn't until eighty or ninety years ago, in fact, that having deacons pass the sacrament became a Churchwide practice.

It's an important duty. When you pass the sacrament, you're doing more than carrying a silver tray around the chapel. You're helping to administer one of the most sacred ordinances in the Church. You're truly serving your Father in Heaven.

Remember that Jesus passed the sacrament to his disciples. Modern-day Apostles pass the sacrament during sacred meetings in the temple. You should feel humbled doing the same thing as an Apostle.

So take your assignment seriously. Treat the sacrament with respect and dignity. Dress nicely and be sure your hands are clean. Be reverent as you walk along the aisles, and whisper if you need to talk. Don't chew gum or candy.

As you pass the sacrament, it's also important to keep your mind focused on worthy thoughts. Think of the Savior, the words to the sacrament hymn, or your favorite scripture or article of faith.

If you have any questions about how you should dress or behave while passing the sacrament, just ask yourself what you'd do if the prophet—or the Savior—were attending your meeting. Then dress and behave accordingly.

Keep in mind that the sacrament is a sacred, holy ordinance. To magnify your calling to help administer the sacrament, you have to treat it solemnly, reverently, and with dignity.

Collecting Fast Offerings

Fast offerings present an excellent opportunity for magnifying your priesthood calling. Unfortunately, some deacons look at collecting fast offerings as a chore rather than as an opportunity to serve their Father in Heaven.

If you want to magnify any calling in the priesthood, start with a good attitude. Remember that when you collect fast offerings you're serving your Father in Heaven. Remember that your efforts bless the lives of many people.

If you keep those things in mind, you will more easily forget the time you're spending away from your home and family.

Another key is to share your good attitude with the people you visit. Smile when you greet them. Introduce yourself whenever you visit someone you don't know, and wipe your feet before entering their home. Because you're representing your Father in Heaven, always be respectful and polite.

Collecting fast offerings can become one of the most enjoyable assignments you have as a deacon. If you tackle your duty with a willing heart and a friendly smile, the work will be easier. Other deacons will be more cheerful too. The time will go by faster and you'll have more fun serving in this way.

Most of all, your Father in Heaven will notice and appreciate your efforts. And you'll be magnifying your priesthood calling.

Caring for Church Facilities

Deacons are expected to help care for Church grounds and buildings. In wards I've attended, elders actually do this more often than deacons. But you can still do your part. Do you ever notice programs left lying around the chapel, for instance?

Pick them up!

Do you ever see bits of litter on the lawn or in the parking lot?

Pick them up!

Do you ever see folding chairs left in the classroom or cultural hall?

Put them away!

Remember that you shouldn't have to be asked to do these things. It doesn't matter if the elders or the priests or even a Primary class have already been asked to do it. Magnifying your calling includes seeing something that needs to be done and then doing your best to do it.

Being a Messenger for the Bishop

When I was a deacon, I was sitting on the front row waiting to pass the sacrament one Sunday when I noticed the bishop motioning for me. A little embarrassed, I crept up to the stand, thinking he was going to tell me to be quiet or something.

Instead, he put his arm around me and whispered, "I'd like you to ask Brother Garrison if the speakers are turned up loud enough."

I looked around. "Where is he?"

The bishop gestured slightly and said, "Clear in the back."

I nodded. "Okay."

Then, tiptoeing down the steps, I went to the back of the building. We had a large ward, and every week the congregation spilled into the cultural hall. Brother Garrison was sitting on the last row.

"The bishop wants to know if the speakers are loud enough back here," I whispered.

He nodded. "Yes, they're fine."

"Okay."

I delivered my message, and the bishop squeezed my shoulder in appreciation. As I walked back to my seat, I suddenly felt a little more important. I felt like I was a part of things.

Delivering messages for the bishop is another part of being a deacon. Some wards even assign a deacon to sit behind the bishop on the stand during sacrament meeting, just in case the bishop needs someone to run an errand in the middle of the meeting.

There are other ways to serve your bishop too. You've probably had the opportunity to deliver flyers around the ward. When you do, don't think of the assignment as a chore. Do your work cheerfully.

I have a friend named Ryan whose ward was planning a youth service project. The deacons were asked to deliver flyers around the ward, not only taking a flyer to each home but also taking the time to explain the project to each family.

"It was a real pain," Ryan said. "Delivering the flyers wasn't that bad, but hardly anyone showed up to help. We only had five deacons to do the whole ward."

"How many deacons are in your quorum?" I asked.

"Twenty-two."

"*Twenty-two?*" I couldn't believe it. Out of twenty-two deacons, only five showed up to help. More to the point, only five were concerned about magnifying their priesthood calling.

Delivering flyers may not be all that fun. It may not seem that important. But when you serve your ward, you're serving your Heavenly Father. You're magnifying your calling.

Remember that it's not *where* you serve in the Church, it's *how* you serve. If you're asked to pass the sacrament, do it well. If you're asked to collect fast offerings, do it cheerfully. If you're asked to deliver flyers, do it willingly.

As you do, you'll become a better deacon. You'll enjoy the blessings of your Father in Heaven. And you'll magnify your priesthood calling.

FIGHTING ON
THE BUS

Chapter Five

Magnifying Your Priesthood Calling as a Teacher

"I can't believe we lost!" Tony Springer slumped in his seat in the back of the bus. "We should have killed those guys!"

"We might have if you could have hit your foul shots," someone snapped.

"Me? I didn't see you scoring a zillion points!" Tony shot back. "And Kyle kept throwing the ball away!"

Kyle Powers sat up in his seat. "I did not!"

"You did too! And K.C. had to go and foul that guy outside the three-point line. *There* were three foul shots we didn't need to give away."

K.C. sat up in his seat. "Hey, shut up, Tony!"

"Come make me!"

"I just might!"

I couldn't believe what was happening. The ninth-grade basketball team had just lost a heartbreaking game in double overtime. The boys had a right to feel bad. But they were going beyond that, attacking one another, blaming each other for the loss.

It was an ugly situation. But right when I thought Tony and K.C. were going to start punching each other, a player named Jerry spoke up.

"Remember Chad's buzzer beater? Now that was sweet!"

"Yeah," someone agreed. "Nothing but net!"

"I felt like Michael Jordan," Chad joked, remembering his last-second prayer shot that knotted the score and sent the game into overtime. "But how 'bout when K.C. hit the ref?"

Everyone laughed. In the first half, K.C. was attempting to lob the ball in bounds when an opposing player swatted it away. The ball ricocheted off the wall and hit the ref in the back of the head, knocking the whistle out of his mouth.

K.C. went red as everyone laughed. But this time everyone was laughing in fun. The meanness and the anger were gone.

With a single question, Jerry had changed the mood of the whole team. Everyone still felt bad about losing, but the friendship was back. The players had quit lashing out at one another.

I remember another time when a similar thing happened. I was guiding a Varsity Scout team on an overnight ski trip. Even though everyone was wearing backpacks—and even though most of the Scouts had never cross-country skied before—most of them were doing great.

A boy named Chris, though, was having a tough time. He fell so often that it wasn't long before everyone was yelling at him.

"C'mon, Chris!" someone would shout. "It's not that hard!"

"Yeah! Get going or get out of the way!"

"At this rate it's going to be midnight before we reach camp!"

Finally, when Chris fell down and had trouble getting back up, everyone was ready to ski off without him. They probably would have, too, if it weren't for Brett.

"My pack's not that heavy," Brett said. "Why don't you let me take your sleeping bag?"

Chris was too tired and frustrated to argue. While he and Brett rearranged their packs, someone else skied up.

"Here, let me take something," he offered.

"Me too," another boy chimed in. "I've got room for something."

Finally, with everyone sharing Chris's load, the group took off again. This time they made good time, and instead of ripping on Chris for having trouble, they were giving him the help and encouragement he needed to keep going.

There are probably times when you too hear people moaning and groaning. Maybe the guys are griping about your new Sunday School teacher. They could be angry at the kid who always has to have his way. Or perhaps they're mad about some activity your advisers have cooked up for next week.

You might even complain once in a while yourself. Or, like Jerry and Brett, maybe you're the one who helps people cool off. Instead of whining when things go wrong, maybe you're the one who points out solutions. Instead of ripping on guys who don't do so well, maybe you're the one who cheers them on.

I hope you are.

Now, you're probably wondering what this has to do with being a teacher. The fact is, teachers are supposed to avoid evil speaking, prevent backbiting, and soothe hard feelings (see D&C 20:53–54). This means that you shouldn't go around complaining about others' shortcomings. Not only should you not gripe and groan about every little thing that goes wrong, you also need to keep others from doing it.

Remember Jerry and Brett? They stopped their friends from getting after one another, and they did it without lecturing, preaching, or getting mad at anyone. They simply turned bad situations into good ones through the power of their examples.

You can do the same thing.

Start with yourself. Make it a habit to look for the good in situations rather than the bad. Focus on people's strengths rather than their weaknesses. Decide that you'll never say anything negative about another person.

Then let your influence spread to others.

Next, learn to be a peacemaker. At home, in school, or in church, whenever you find yourself in a situation where the tension is thick and feelings are strained, help everyone cool off. Instead of being someone who fuels the fire, be the one who makes peace.

As you do these things, three things will happen: you'll earn the respect of the people around you, you'll prevent countless ulcers, and you'll magnify your priesthood calling.

When you become a teacher, you still have all of the authority of a deacon. You can still perform all of the duties of a deacon. So be willing to help pass the sacrament or collect fast offerings if you're needed.

Remember that these are not chores you get out of by becoming a teacher. They are important duties. To magnify your calling in the priesthood, you must perform them cheerfully.

Preparing the Sacrament

On most Sundays, you'll be able to help prepare the sacrament. Before you do, be sure to wash your hands. This is not only because people are going to eat and drink the bread and water, but also because these emblems represent the body and blood of our Savior. They deserve your respect.

After the meeting, clear the sacrament table reverently, being respectful of the trays, tablecloth, and any bread or water that's left over. Don't simply pile the trays back in the closet; take the time to clean them thoroughly. Stack them carefully as you put them away. Fold the tablecloth neatly.

To honor the Savior—and to magnify your priesthood calling—you must treat the sacrament with respect, reverence, and dignity.

Acting as an Usher

In many wards, teachers are also expected to be ushers.

I was once asked to speak in a sacrament meeting in a town several miles away. I got lost on the way and didn't find the chapel until after the meeting had started.

Trying to be as quiet as I could, I tiptoed in the door. The ward choir was seated in the stands, and I was looking for a place to sit when someone tapped me on the arm.

"Hi," he whispered. "Can I help you find someone?"

I turned to find a teenage boy standing beside me. He was wearing a nice suit, his hair was combed neatly, and he was smiling politely. On his coat was a button that said *Usher*.

I shook his hand. "I'm supposed to give a talk," I whispered. "I guess I took a wrong turn somewhere."

His smile grew wide. "Oh, yeah! Bishop Smart told me to watch for you."

With that, he led me to a seat, then walked up to the stand to tell the bishop I'd arrived.

I'm usually nervous before I speak anyway, but because I was late that day my nervous system was tied up in knots. But the young teacher's friendliness calmed me down and made me feel good. He made me feel happy I was there.

At the time, I couldn't help thinking about other ushers I'd seen: boys who rock back and forth in their chairs, frowning every time anyone goes in or out.

Like most things, your attitude is important. If you're going to be an usher—if you're going to represent your ward as an official greeter—do your job seriously.

Assisting the Bishop

Teachers are also expected to help the bishop in his role of administering the temporal affairs of the ward. In the last chapter I mentioned the bad winter of 1993. You might remember it. I do because one night it snowed so deep that I got my car stuck in my own driveway. No sooner did I dig it out than a snowplow came by and piled a mound of snow back in front of it.

I happen to live by a fifteen-year-old teacher named Brian. After shoveling his own walks, he attacked the driveway of Sister Lloyd, an elderly woman who lived next door. He cleaned the walks and cleared a path from her driveway into the street. Then he climbed her house and shoveled the snow off the roof.

I know that shoveling walks and mowing lawns for the elderly is a bit of a cliché. But Sister Lloyd had no one else to do it for her. By shoveling her walks, Brian blessed her life.

You can bless the lives of others too. If you have neighbors who need help shoveling their walks or mowing their lawns, help them! If you know someone who needs a hand raking the leaves or weeding the garden, give them a hand!

Not only will you bless their lives, but you'll please your Father in Heaven. And you'll magnify your priesthood calling.

Strengthening the Church

According to the Doctrine and Covenants, the Lord expects teachers to "watch over the church always, and be with and strengthen them" (D&C 20:53). If you're like most fourteen- and fifteen-year-olds, you might have a hard time understanding what this means, even though it's one of the most exciting things about being a teacher.

Let me give you an example.

When I was fifteen, our quorum was once asked to pull weeds at the stake welfare farm. It was dull, boring work. We'd been at it for about an hour (it seemed more like a year!), and I was stretching a kink out of my back, when my friend Cannon pedaled up and jumped off his bike.

"Hi, guys!" he shouted. "Having fun?"

Someone threw a clump of weeds at him. But Cannon charged into the work with a barrage of jokes and stories, and suddenly pulling weeds wasn't boring anymore. Cannon's energy, enthusiasm, and zany sense of humor recharged us. With him helping out, the next hour flew by—and farm work actually became kind of fun!

Like Cannon, you can be a strength to your quorum. You can be the spark that keeps your family, friends, and neighbors fired up. You can be the boost people need when they're down.

How?

Consider these ideas:

1. Be cheerful. When the day is cold and the job is hard, there's nothing like a cheerful laugh and a friendly smile to keep people happy. Be the person with that laugh and smile.
2. Be optimistic. Attitudes are contagious, so be certain that yours is always positive. If you always look for the bright side of things, others will be more likely to do so too.
3. Look for opportunities to help others. If you see someone having a bad day, give him a pat on the back. Do something to cheer him up. Find a way to get him back on track. Go out of your way to make a difference in his life.
4. Share your testimony. As young men grow older, many become inactive. Some struggle with their testimonies. Others decide not to serve missions.

    By sharing your testimony and setting a proper example, you can help keep them on the right track. So if you have friends who are not as active as they should be, invite them to activities! If you know people who struggle with their testimonies, share yours! If you know someone who's worried about serving a mission, get him excited!

    The time will come when each man will have to stand on the strength of his own testimony. You can help your friends prepare by strengthening them now.

Your duties as a teacher go far beyond preparing the sacrament. You can make a real difference in the lives of the people around you.

Decide that you'll do it! Fulfill your duties faithfully, and you'll earn the respect of your friends and family. You'll earn the blessings of your Father in Heaven. And you'll magnify your priesthood.

STRANDED ON
THE LAKE

Chapter Six

*Magnifying Your Priesthood Calling
as a Priest*

Corey Mitchell dipped his oar in the lake and stroked, pushing his father's boat slowly through the water. "Okay, I've got one," he said. "Cats always land on their feet, right?"

Tim Slater, Jennifer Nuttall, and Erica Wilson nodded their heads. "Right."

"And toast always lands with the buttered side down, right?"

"Right."

Corey shrugged. "So what happens if you strap a piece of toast to the back of a cat?"

Everyone laughed as Corey once again dug his paddle deep into the lake and pulled.

"And—oh, yeah!" he said as something occurred to him. "How 'bout this: if you spill detergent all over the floor, is the floor clean or dirty?"

Everyone laughed again. Corey took a moment to stretch his arms, and Tim took the oar from him.

"Want me to spell you for a minute?"

"Yeah, thanks."

Corey sat back in the boat and stared out across the lake. Far in the distance he could see the tops of sailboats near the Provo boat harbor. But they were too far away to signal.

Corey didn't say anything, but he was worried. He and Tim had invited Jennifer and Erica to spend the afternoon with them on his father's boat. After racing the boat around Utah Lake and taking turns water-skiing, the four teenagers found a remote corner of the lake and had a picnic on the water. It had been a great afternoon. But when it came time to leave and Corey tried to start the engine . . . nothing happened.

He frowned, glanced at Tim, then tried the key again. Again, nothing.

"Uh-oh," he said. "I don't think I like this."

He and Tim had fiddled around with the engine for a few minutes, but neither of them knew much about mechanics and nothing they did helped.

Finally, Corey had pulled out the emergency oar and begun paddling.

"I knew it was silly to think we could paddle our way in," he told me later. "I mean, we were miles away from the harbor. But I had to do something."

Normally, being stranded on the lake might have been a little inconvenient, but not especially dangerous. On this day, though, the wind began picking up. The boat rose and fell on two- and three-foot waves, and there was no way to signal for help.

Corey was worried, but he didn't share his fears with his passengers. Instead, as the sun sank deeper into the horizon, he tried to keep their spirits up by telling them jokes and amusing them with his favorite "ponderables."

"Have you ever heard of jumbo shrimp?" he asked. "What is that, anyway? Big shrimp or baby jumbos?"

"I've got one," Jennifer said. "You know how at school—"

"Shhhh!" Corey said, holding up his hand and cutting her off. "Listen."

Everyone listened. At first, no one could hear anything but the sound of the waves lapping against the boat. Corey was beginning to think he was imagining things, but then it came again. He could just make out a soft murmur like the rumble of distant thunder. But he knew it wasn't thunder. *It was a motor!*

Leaping to his feet, Corey looked around, then jumped on top of the engine housing. Right away he spotted a boat over the whitecaps. He grabbed a life jacket and waved it over his head.

"Here!" he shouted. "Over here!"

A moment later the boat turned in his direction. Corey and his friends erupted in a roar of cheers and hugs.

"It was the last boat off the lake," Corey told me later. "And it towed us back in." He grinned. "Man, that boat was the most beautiful thing I've ever seen in my life!"

But the story doesn't end there. A couple of days later, Corey was working on his homework when the phone rang.

It was Jennifer's father.

"I wanted to thank you for taking care of my daughter," he said. "Jennifer told me all about it. She told me how you took care of everyone, and how you kept everyone from worrying. I want you to know how much it means to my wife and me that Jennifer has friends like you."

Wouldn't it be great if the parents of the girls you date

felt like that about you? Actually, if you're magnifying your priesthood calling, many parents will feel that way. They'll know by your actions, your example, and your attitude that you're a fine young man. They'll know that their daughter will be safe with you.

Becoming a priest is an exciting thing. Because you're sixteen, in most states you're finally old enough to drive. You're old enough to get a part-time job. And—yes— you're finally old enough to date.

When you're ordained a priest, you receive special privileges. You receive the same priesthood that John the Baptist used to baptize the Savior. You receive the authority to baptize, confer the Aaronic Priesthood, and bless the sacrament.

But along with these blessings come special duties and obligations, and magnifying your priesthood calling takes on new dimensions. Especially in your relationships with young women. Be sure that you treat them right! In all of your relationships with young women, be certain that you conduct yourself so that they know you honor them and the priesthood you bear. This is important for two reasons: (1) the Lord expects you to respect women for one thing, and (2) when you're a priest, you need to prepare yourself for your mission; you need to keep yourself clean and worthy.

So as you begin dating, keep these tips in mind:

- Double- and triple-date whenever you can. Having your friends and their dates along not only makes an evening more fun but also helps you resist temptations.

- Attend appropriate activities. This doesn't mean that every date has to be a Church fireside. But you don't want to spend all your time at drive-in movies either. Instead, look for activities where you can talk, laugh, and get to know one another.

- Don't stay out too late. Especially on school nights, it's important that you return your date home at a reasonable hour. But it's important on weekends too. Not only do temptations become more difficult to resist late at night, but being able to wake up refreshed on Sunday morning is an important part of keeping the Sabbath holy.

  Remember that if you need to be out later than you expected, be sure to phone your date's parents, as well as your own.

- Be fun to date! You don't have to be the best-looking guy in the school, and you don't need to drive the nicest car. But if you treat your dates like they're special, they'll enjoy going out with you.

Blessing the Sacrament

When you consider the duties of a priest, one of the first things you probably think of is administering the sacrament. What an important duty! The sacrament is one of the most sacred, holy ordinances in the Church. It's more than simply breaking slices of bread and repeating a couple of prayers. It's symbolic of the body and blood of our Savior, and the sacrifice he made for us.

Because the sacrament is so sacred, you must do your part to invite the Spirit of the Lord as you officiate at the sacrament table. Follow these suggestions:

1. Be worthy. When you bless the sacrament, you are acting on behalf of the entire congregation. Be

certain that you're worthy of doing that! Be sure
that your heart and hands are clean.
2. Dress appropriately. Wear a white shirt and tie if you
have them.
3. Conduct yourself with dignity. Sit up straight while
you're at the sacrament table. Don't joke, whisper,
or fidget.
4. Offer the prayer solemnly. The sacrament prayer is
so sacred that it must be recited precisely. Don't
rush through it! Remember that you're not simply
reciting words, you're offering a sacred prayer to
your Heavenly Father.

To pray effectively, you should understand what
you're praying for. Take the time to study both of the
sacrament prayers. Read the words carefully. Analyze
them. Strive to understand what you're saying, and it
will be easier to offer a sincere, heartfelt prayer.

Remember that as a priest, you can still perform all the
duties of deacons and teachers. So be ready to step in if
there are not enough young men to prepare or pass the
sacrament. Keep in mind that these are important responsibilities: don't treat them lightly.

When I was a missionary in Japan, I often served in
wards and branches where there weren't any Aaronic
Priesthood bearers. So I was often asked to prepare, bless,
and pass the sacrament . . . sometimes all in the same
meeting!

What surprised me, though, was how much I enjoyed
doing that. Each week I looked forward to helping with the
sacrament.

You should have the same attitude. Whether you're
officiating at the sacrament table or helping the deacons
and teachers, do it gratefully and willingly.

Teaching the Gospel

As a priest, you also have the duty to preach, teach, expound, and exhort (see D&C 20:46). This includes such things as doing home teaching and working with full-time missionaries when you have the chance. Taking advantage of these opportunities will not only help you to magnify your calling, but will also help you prepare for your mission.

Remember, though, that you can teach more by the way you act than you ever can by what you say. So be your own best lesson! Actively live the gospel. Be clean in word and deed. Make it clear to everyone around you that you're a faithful bearer of the priesthood.

While you're at it, be sure that everyone knows you're preparing yourself to serve a mission too. You may not realize it, but your example will influence young men who might still be debating whether to serve a mission.

Your example will also have a powerful impact on the deacons and teachers in the ward. You'd be surprised to learn how many young men will pattern themselves after you. They'll see the way you do things, and they'll in turn do them the same way.

So let them see your enthusiasm for missionary work. Help get them excited. Encourage them to begin preparing themselves.

When you become a priest, you near the end of your experiences in the Aaronic Priesthood. Your time of preparation is almost over. So make the most of it! Maintain the sacred nature of the sacrament by keeping yourself worthy to officiate at the sacrament table. Offer the sacrament prayers reverently and with dignity. Teach the gospel, not only in quorum meeting and by home teaching but also by setting an example of righteousness to those around you. Be your own best lesson.

Finally, respect the young women in your life. Let them know by the way you act that you honor your priesthood.

As you do these things, you'll prepare yourself to receive the Melchizedek Priesthood. You'll be able to charge into your mission with confidence. And you'll magnify your priesthood calling to heights you never believed possible.

TEACHING WITH MR. DAVIS

Chapter Seven

*Magnifying Your Priesthood Calling
Through Home Teaching*

"Whoa, whoa, whoaaaa. . . ."

Mr. Davis frowned as he waved the band quiet. He waited until everyone had put down their instruments, then lifted his baton.

"Trumpets . . . concert B-flat."

I was sitting in the middle of the trumpet section. Feeling sheepish at being the only instrument section in trouble, we lifted our trumpets and tried to sound as good as possible.

It didn't work.

Mr. Davis wrinkled his nose like he'd just had a whiff of something old and moldy.

"Whew!" he said, shaking his head and walking toward us. "Someone's hurting my ears. Let's try it one at a time."

He had each of us play until he identified the trouble-maker and tuned him up. He lifted his baton.

"Now, let's try it again."

We played again, this time hitting the note perfectly. Mr. Davis smiled.

"Good. That's much better."

He began walking back to the podium, but suddenly and turned and pointed his baton at me.

"By the way, Shane, we've been assigned to be home-teaching companions. I'll give you a call tonight and we'll set something up."

My heart skipped a beat as Mr. Davis strolled away. My eyes bugged out. My jaw dropped and my face flushed as everyone around me snickered.

My friend Gary leaned over and nudged me with his elbow. "You're going to be companions with *Mr. Davis?*" He chuckled. "Good luck!"

I couldn't believe it. Mr. Davis wasn't my favorite teacher. And I'm sure I wasn't his favorite student. I certainly wasn't one of his best musicians.

But home-teaching companions?

I shuddered.

It was hard to picture. Actually, it was hard to picture doing home teaching at all. I was a high school junior and had just turned sixteen. I had never been home teaching with anyone before, and I couldn't remember the last time home teachers had visited my family.

I was sure I wasn't going to like it.

It wasn't long, though, before I realized that when it came to home teaching, Mr. Davis was like someone straight out of the *New Era*. He was awesome. We taught two families, and he loved and cared about them. He knew not only the names of all the children in both families but also who their schoolteachers were, what subjects they were best at, and what their talents, interests, and hobbies were.

What really impressed me was that Mr. Davis cared about me too. He went the extra mile to make certain I felt included. He made sure I knew I was needed. He let me know that I was an important part of the team.

When I was in high school I belonged to an archery club and often competed in tournaments all over the state. One month, Mr. Davis asked me to bring my archery equipment on our home teaching visits. After I'd shown off my bow and arrows, he gave a lesson on goals and keeping our lives "on target."

I know this will sound corny, but with Mr. Davis as my companion it wasn't long before I actually looked forward to going home teaching.

That was my first experience with home teaching. I'm happy it was a good one because I've been doing it ever since. I've learned that quality home teaching is a way of magnifying your priesthood calling, and it's one of the most important things you can ever do in the Church.

When I was on my mission in Japan, I was once transferred to a tiny mountain town. My new companion told me that among other things, we were responsible for making home teaching visits to inactive members.

I was a brand-new senior companion, raring to baptize everyone in sight. I didn't realize that visiting inactive members was not one of the more popular assignments in the ward.

"All right!" I said. "That's great. We'll go meet 'em all tonight and invite 'em to church!"

My companion rolled his eyes. What he didn't tell me was that he'd visited most of our families before and that they weren't excited about seeing missionaries.

We took off and found the home of Yamaguchi-san.

"I moved here from Tokyo two years ago," he told us. "And I just never got around to going to church again."

I quickly wrote down the address of the ward meeting-house and invited him out. He accepted.

That Sunday, Yamaguchi-san came to church. He came the next week, too. And before I transferred, he was called to be secretary in the elders quorum. The elders quorum president invited me to stand in the circle when they set him apart.

That was exciting for me because I had never baptized anyone during my whole mission. Yamaguchi-san was my first success as a missionary, and it was the result of a home teaching visit.

Now, you're going to have opportunities to do home teaching too. While you hold the Aaronic Priesthood, you will probably serve as a junior companion. But you can still be a great home teacher. By doing so, not only will you be serving your Father in Heaven but you will be blessing the lives of others. And you will be magnifying your priesthood calling.

Let's look at a couple of ways of doing that.

Understand Your Calling

To be an effective home teacher, you have to understand the divine nature of your job. Rather than a home *teacher*, think of yourself as a family *guardian*. Your duty is more important than simply delivering a message each month. It means being concerned with the family's welfare.

I once went with my teachers quorum to Lake Powell for a week. As soon as we got there, our adviser assigned each of us a buddy and gave us an ironclad rule.

"No one goes anywhere," he said, "without his buddy. And you are each responsible for your buddy's safety."

In a way, that's what home teaching is all about—watching out for one another.

Think of it this way: Your bishop is responsible for the welfare of every family in the ward. But he can't personally visit every family each month to make certain that everything is all right, so he counts on you to keep a prayerful, watchful eye on certain families. He counts on you to support and encourage them, to watch for problems, and to let him know when a family needs his help.

Remember that being a home teacher is a calling of service. Sincerely look for ways to bless the lives of those you teach. Many home teachers end their visit by asking, "Is there anything we can do for you?" And most people respond by saying something like, "Well, no, not that we can think of."

As guardian of a family, though, don't simply ask to help. Look for ways you can be of service.

When I was seventeen, I was driving to work one afternoon when I saw Brother Dixon walking down the road. He was the father of one of the families I taught with Mr. Davis.

I pulled over and asked if he needed a ride.

"Oh, you saved my life," he said as he climbed in the car. "I have to be at work in ten minutes and my wife has the car."

A couple of months later, I was doing my homework when Brother Dixon called.

"I've got a class at BYU tonight," he said, "and my wife has the car again. Is there any chance you could give me a ride?"

"Sure," I said. "I'll be right over."

Driving to BYU only took a few minutes. But as I dropped him off, I remember feeling good that Brother Dixon had felt comfortable enough to ask me for a ride.

Many people will be reluctant to ask you for help, even when they need it. But when they come to know that you are willing to help them, they'll become more open.

More important, they'll be more willing to call when they need help of a more spiritual nature.

Remember that when you're serving others, you're serving your Father in Heaven.

Support Your Companion

Many young men your age get to go home teaching with their fathers. And that's great. There's nothing as powerful as being able to join forces with your father in a priesthood activity.

Many times, though, you might be asked to be companions with another man who holds the Melchizedek Priesthood. This will give you the opportunity to work with and learn from someone else.

Enjoy the experience!

If you truly love your companion, the people you teach will feel it. And they'll respond. Just as important, the Lord will bless you for your efforts.

Remember that being a junior companion doesn't mean sitting around and waiting for your companion to make all of the decisions. Instead, help him. Support him. Learn from him. Do what you can to make his job easier.

One way you can do this is by taking your turn teaching lessons and bearing your testimony. You can also help by offering to make appointments, making yourself available for visits, and honoring his decisions.

Take Your Turn Teaching Lessons

Even though you're young, you have a lot to contribute. You have a powerful, energetic spirit, and you can bless the lives of the families you teach. You have the ability to inspire kids your own age, adults, and even the youngest children in the family.

Don't be afraid to take your turn teaching the lesson. In fact, don't wait to be asked. Volunteer! Offer to teach the lesson every other month.

Then, when your turn comes, do your best to present a good, meaningful lesson. After consulting with your companion, prayerfully choose a topic. Use the Church magazines for ideas. Think back to spiritual experiences you've had. Search the scriptures. After you've settled on a topic, find ways of relating it to the family you're teaching. Make your lesson come to life.

Finally, whether you or your companion is presenting the lesson, be sure to share your testimony.

Remember that presenting lessons will not only help you to be a better home teacher, it will help you to magnify your priesthood calling and prepare you for your mission.

Become Friends with the Families You Teach

You should strive to become friends with the families you teach for at least two reasons. First, when they feel that your friendship and interest are genuine, they'll be more receptive to your message. They'll be more willing to open up to you.

Second, the more you know about them, the better you'll be able to understand their needs.

When I was in college, my home teachers happened to be my best friends. One afternoon I was finishing up my homework when they came over. We talked about girls, school, jobs, and everything else that was going on in our lives.

After an hour or so, Leon looked at his watch.

"Wow," he said. "We'd better go. I've got to work tonight." Then he looked at me and asked, "Who would you like to pray, me or Greg?"

I started to laugh. "Pray? You mean this is a home teaching visit?"

He nodded, and the three of us burst out laughing. It seemed funny at the time, but in an ideal world, maybe that's the way home teaching would be. You would be so close to the people you teach that they'd never know the difference between official and unofficial visits.

You can start by going out of your way to shake hands and say hi to them in church. Remember their birthdays with cards or phone calls. Take interest in their careers, hobbies, talents, and interests. Find out what motivates their lives.

When I was teaching with Mr. Davis, we were once assigned to visit Brother and Sister Tischner, an elderly couple whose children had moved away. As soon as Brother Tischner learned that I liked archery, he took me to a back room where he had an assortment of bows, arrows, and spears he had collected in Africa. It was incredible!

I never had any idea that I could have something in common with a seventy-five-year-old man, but after that night we never ran out of things to talk about.

You can do the same thing. Really get to know the people you're assigned to visit. Then, as your friendship grows, you'll be able to bless their lives in ways you never dreamed possible.

Home teaching is one of the most important callings you'll ever have in the Church, so don't look at it as a chore that keeps you from being out with your friends. Look at it as a way to bless others, a chance to serve your Father in Heaven, and an opportunity to magnify your priesthood calling.

Be faithful in your calling. Support your companion and take your turn presenting lessons. Become close to the families you teach and earnestly strive to serve them.

As you do you'll be blessed, not only now but for eternities to come.

CALLED
TO SERVE!

Chapter Eight

Serving in Your Quorum Presidency

Travis Rimmer had just been set apart as the first counselor in his deacons quorum. The unusual thing was that he'd also been set apart as the quorum secretary.

"We only had three deacons in our whole ward," he explained. "So my friend Jon was called to be president, and he recommended me as his first counselor *and* secretary."

Travis said that after he was set apart, he asked the bishop if having two jobs meant he was going to get twice as many blessings.

"That all depends," the bishop replied with a wink, "on if you do twice as much work."

One of the most exciting things about the Aaronic Priesthood is that the Lord allows young men your age to preside over their quorums. He gives them trust, authority, and inspiration, just as he does to men presiding over

Melchizedek Priesthood quorums. He gives them all the keys they need to serve their brethren and lead their quorums.

What a great opportunity! There are few organizations that give young men such great trust and responsibility. You might be captain of your baseball team, for instance, but your coach still calls the plays. And you might be president of your school, but your principal still makes the rules.

When you are called to be president of your Aaronic Priesthood quorum, though, the Lord expects you to call the shots. He expects you to make the decisions. He expects you to take charge.

Now, you probably think that's great. And it is! But along with being a great blessing, being president of a quorum is a tremendous responsibility. It means you are accountable to your Heavenly Father for your quorum's success. It means you are responsible for helping others to gain strong testimonies. It means you are accountable for keeping the members of your quorum strong and active in the Church.

If you fulfill your duties faithfully, the Lord will bless you. You'll acquire leadership skills that will bless you at school, on your mission, and through your whole life.

Here's how to get started:

Choose Your Counselors Prayerfully

When you are called to be president of your quorum, the bishop will ask you to recommend other young men to be your counselors and secretary. This will be your first duty as president, and your decisions will have long-lasting consequences. Make your choices carefully.

Start by considering each member of your quorum.

Identify which young men will give you the best support, assistance, and counsel. Look for those who will help you make good decisions. Identify those who will serve your quorum faithfully.

Remember that this is not a popularity contest. You're not deciding which of the guys are your best friends: you're choosing those who will do the best job.

After considering each person, make a decision. Then share your thoughts with the Lord. Pray earnestly, telling your Heavenly Father whom you have selected and asking him if your decision is right. Have faith that he will confirm whether you have made the right decision.

I know a young man named Justin who was called to be president of his teachers quorum. He reviewed the names of everyone in the quorum, and he knew whom he wanted to recommend as his first counselor and secretary. But he couldn't come to a decision about his second counselor.

"I thought and thought and thought," he told me. "And I prayed and prayed and prayed. But I just couldn't figure it out. No one I thought about seemed right."

But then it hit him. A boy named Russ had just moved into the ward. Justin hadn't met Russ, but as soon as Russ's name came to mind Justin knew he had his second counselor. He visited the bishop and made his recommendation.

"I haven't met Russ," the bishop said. "What's he like?"

"I don't know," Justin admitted. "I haven't met him either."

The bishop blinked. "You haven't met him? But you want him to be your counselor?"

"Yes," Justin insisted. "I feel really good about it."

The bishop nodded and said it would be a good idea to meet Russ anyway . . . just to be certain. So Justin went to Russ's home and introduced himself.

"As soon as I met him I knew I'd made the right deci-sion," Justin said. "Russ was great. We hit it right off, and he was an awesome counselor."

Again, remember that choosing your counselors is more than simply picking out your best friends. The Lord is trusting you to select the best leaders for the quorum. Be thoughtful. Be prayerful. Choose young men who will as-sist you and serve your quorum well.

Work Closely with Your Adviser

Presiding over an Aaronic Priesthood quorum is an awesome responsibility. You have counselors and a secre-tary to help you, of course. And you also have an adult ad-viser, who will offer as much guidance and counsel as you need to be effective.

Remember that your adviser is one of your most valu-able resources. As a Melchizedek Priesthood bearer, he has a lot of experience, so listen closely to his advice and coun-sel. Ask him whenever you need ideas for activities, for making quorum meetings more interesting, or for working with inactive members. After all, he's probably faced many of the same challenges you will, and he'll often have ideas for dealing with them.

Finally, remember that the Lord called him to be your adviser. The Lord wants him to work with you. Be sure to treat him accordingly.

Preside over Your Quorum

In some wards, adult advisers simply take charge of Aaronic Priesthood quorums, even though that's the job of the youth presidency. Many times this is because the youth leaders don't, won't, or can't do it themselves.

But if the Lord called you to preside over a quorum, that's what he expects you to do. So do it! Take charge in quorum and presidency meetings. Get things under control. Follow an agenda. Organize activities and delegate responsibilities. Do the job the Lord called you to do.

This might be hard to do at first. After all, you might not have much leadership experience. But the Lord chose you, and he has confidence in you. He knows you can do it. Don't worry about your shortcomings—just go for it! Charge into your work with enthusiasm and confidence. *Learn by experience* to be a great leader.

If you ever need help or have questions, talk with your adviser. After all, that's what he's there for. Remember that your bishop or bishopric counselor is available, too, if you need him. Finally, stay close to your Heavenly Father through prayer, and seek the guidance of the Holy Ghost.

Lead As the Savior Led

I remember watching a certain college basketball game. It was a great game, but the best part was watching the visiting coach. He stood on the sideline the entire game yelling, pointing, and shouting orders.

Then, anytime one of the officials made a bad call, the coach went crazy, waving his arms and shouting like the end of the world had come. He was so wild that it wasn't long before one of the refs gave him a technical foul. Then, in the second half, they tossed him out of the game.

Later, I couldn't help thinking that in today's world, many leaders are just like that. They shout and yell, giving orders and commands and expecting everyone to do what they say.

But that's not the Lord's way. Jesus led by example. He led by serving others. And so should you.

In the Church, being a leader means being a servant. As a member of your quorum presidency, you're not called to be bossy. You are called to serve. You're called to help the members of your quorum grow in the priesthood.

Start by loving each member of your quorum. Be tolerant of their weaknesses and shortcomings. Search for ways to keep each person active and to help them magnify their priesthood calling.

Next, set a proper example. If you want the quorum members to be reverent during quorum meeting, be reverent yourself. If you want them to volunteer for assignments, be sure you volunteer yourself. Nothing you teach will ever influence others as much as the power of your own example.

Finally, be patient. No one is perfect, and no matter what you do, your fellow quorum members are going to mess up once in a while. When they do, don't blow up. Instead, count to ten, take a couple of deep breaths, and ask yourself, "What would Jesus do?" Then act accordingly.

Teach Your Quorum Members Their Duty

One of the most important things you can ever do as a member of your quorum presidency is to teach your brethren to honor and magnify their priesthood callings. Start by visiting each young man as he joins the quorum. Make him feel welcome. Explain what his assignments will be.

Then, in quorum meetings, help everyone to understand exactly what their duties are. Explain exactly what it takes to fulfill those duties.

If you are a deacon, for instance, explain what it means to be a messenger for the bishop, and give examples. If you're a teacher, explain what it means to be a strength to the Church. Again, give examples. Share ideas. Challenge everyone to follow through.

Watch Over Your Quorum

When you are called to lead a quorum, you take on the responsibility of watching over your brethren. This means understanding each person's special needs and challenges. It means helping members who are struggling. It means assisting those who need help or encouragement.

Start by getting to know each person in your quorum. Become friends with them. Discover their talents, strengths, and weaknesses. Find out what really makes them tick.

Then watch out for them. If Jon begins skipping activities, devise special events to get his interest back. If Steve starts hanging out with the school hoods, go out of your way to spend time with him. Show him that he has other friends to choose from.

And if anyone has special challenges—such as problems at home or with the Word of Wisdom—seek the guidance of your quorum adviser and bishopric member.

Be careful as you do these things. Don't talk about anyone in ways that might appear gossipy, and don't share personal or embarrassing details of their lives with other members of your quorum.

Support Your Leaders

One of the first things you'll learn as president of your quorum is that you can't succeed without support. After all, if no one cooperates in quorum meetings, shows up for assignments, or participates in activities, you won't *have* a quorum.

So when you are called to be a counselor or assistant in your quorum presidency, set an example by supporting and sustaining your ward and quorum leaders. Be enthusiastic about programs and activities they come up with. Be faith-ful in attending activities. Give your leaders the same sup-port and loyalty you would like to receive yourself.

Learning to be a good leader will help prepare you for your mission. Your experiences will help prepare you for your career. They'll help prepare you to one day preside over a ward, stake, or mission.

Who knows? They might even be preparing you to pre-side over the Church. That's why it's important that you do the best job you can. Learn to lead as the Savior led, strengthen your quorum, and teach your brethren their duties. Your Heavenly Father will notice your efforts, and you'll develop leadership skills that will bless and serve you for the rest of your life.

CLIMBING
THE CRACK

Chapter Nine

Magnifying Your Priesthood Calling Through Scouting

"Tension!"

David Knapp jammed his boot into a crack and flattened himself against the rock as he tried to keep his balance. His fingers were gripping bumps no larger than cherries as he clung to the face.

"Hang on, Dave!" someone shouted. "You can do it!"

Dave scanned the rock above him, then inched his way up. He climbed a foot or two, then stopped and mopped his forehead with a flannel shirtsleeve.

"Over to your left!" someone shouted. "There's a big crack!"

Dave reached out with his free hand. "Over here?"

"No! The other way!"

Dave slid his hand over the rock, finding the crack and

slipping his fingers inside. He took a deep breath, then pulled himself up the rock.

Dave was a member of my Varsity Scout Team, and we were visiting the mountaineering outpost at the Beaver High Adventure Base. We had spent the morning rappelling down the camp's sheer lava cliffs, and now we were taking turns "climbing the crack."

From the bottom, it didn't look that tough. After all, the crack ran the entire length of the cliff, and everyone was tied to a safety line to keep from falling.

Once you got on the rock, though, everything changed. Holes that looked perfect for grabbing turned out to be too shallow. Bumps that seemed perfect for standing on suddenly became too smooth.

Dave was just figuring that out. Halfway up, he scanned the rock for finger holds, finally spotting another good crack a few feet to his right. Getting there would be dicey.

"Tension!" he yelled again.

"Tension!" his safety man repeated, taking in slack on the rope. Now, if Dave slipped, the rope would catch him before he could fall. Dave took a moment to gather his courage, then suddenly darted across the face, clinging to the rock like Spiderman. His boot slipped once, then stopped.

He'd made it.

Dave took a moment to catch his breath and pose for a picture, then scrambled the rest of the way up the rock.

It was my turn next, and I could feel my heart pounding in my chest as I cinched up my helmet. Even so, I couldn't help but think how much fun I was having. This was our third day at Beaver, and we were having a blast. We'd spent the day before canoeing, sailing, and swimming in Three Creeks Reservoir. The day before that we'd fired

black-powder rifles at the mountain man outpost. And to-
morrow we were going to help build a log cabin at the base
lumberjack camp.

It was one of the best weeks of my life.

But then Scouting is like that. Good Scouting programs are filled with fun, excitement, and adventure. But
there's a serious side, too. Scouting teaches you to cultivate
clean thoughts and actions. It helps you to show love and
respect to your family. It teaches you to keep your mind
and body clean and to live a better life.

Remember David and Goliath? What a mismatch!
David was a small, teenage boy, while Goliath was a mon-
ster ten feet tall. The tip of his spear alone weighed eighteen pounds.

He would have scared Rambo!

But David had the right weapons. With a leather sling,
a few stones, and a little know-how, he slew Goliath. The
scriptures don't tell us where David learned to use his
slingshot, but I believe that today, that's the sort of thing a
boy might learn in Scouting.

You see, you face Goliaths of your own every day.
Scouting gives you the weapons you need to beat them.
That's one of the reasons that in many places, Scouting is
an officially approved Church activity. It's linked to the
Aaronic Priesthood program.

In other words, when you're doing your best in
Scouting, you're magnifying your priesthood calling.

Think about that for a minute. You get to go hiking,
camping, and swimming, and you get blessed for it! It's like
being paid to go to a ball game!

Another nice thing about Scouting is that when you
belong to a good troop, Varsity Team, or Explorer Post, you
not only learn valuable skills but you also have a great time
doing it. My own Scouting adventures have included flying

airplanes, rappeling from cliffs, exploring caves, and rafting rivers. Those experiences have been among the highlights of my life.

So if your ward has a Scouting program, take advantage of it! Have fun! Remember that when you're doing your best in Scouting, you are magnifying your priesthood calling. And to do your best, keep the following in mind.

Earn Your Eagle

The Boy Scout program was designed to promote citizenship, physical fitness, and character development. One of the ways it does that is through rank advancement.

In other words, climbing the ranks from First Class to Star, and then from Life to Eagle is not just something for your mother and Scoutmaster to bug you about. It's what Scouting is all about.

Unfortunately, not everyone realizes that. Few young men ever earn their Eagle.

But if you want to magnify your priesthood calling, be one of the few who do. Make it a goal. Pick a date no more than a year from now (yes, you can do it that fast), write it down, and post it someplace where you'll see it often.

Next, list everything you'll need to accomplish between now and then. Write down each of the merit badges you'll need to earn. Organize a plan to complete them before your target date.

Then go for it! Keep after it! Do your best to follow through.

If you're not clear about what you need to do, talk with your Scoutmaster. And if you belong to a troop where advancement isn't emphasized, seek help from your friends, older Eagle Scouts in the ward, or professionals at your local Scout office.

Choose a Good Eagle Project

One of the last things you need to do to earn your Eagle is complete a project. Choose a good one. Find something that's meaningful, something that will benefit your community and that you can look back on with pride.

I have a friend named Tom who (with the help of his troop) planted more than five thousand Ponderosa pine trees in a canyon that had been burned off in a forest fire.

I know another young man named Bryan who lives for baseball. His town had a nice ballpark, but no bleachers. So he convinced local businessmen to donate the lumber, then built two sets of bleachers.

The nice thing about both of these projects is that they were needed and that they blessed many people. Tom's project beautified a whole mountain, and Bryan's bleachers are filled every afternoon all summer long.

Another benefit is that both Tom and Bryan will see their projects for years to come. They'll remind both boys of their service to their communities.

Be sure that your project is just as meaningful.

Visit with your Scoutmaster or contact your local Scout office if you need specific suggestions for projects.

Help Other Scouts

As you work toward your Eagle, you will learn many things. You can then help your troop by sharing your skills with younger Scouts as they join up.

Many wards actually develop a leadership corps and have older Scouts assist the Scoutmaster in meetings and on campouts. But even if your ward doesn't have such a program, you can still help out. Volunteer to help with special activities or attend campouts.

Then, if you are invited to help, be sure that you're actually helping. Do what you can to make the Scoutmaster's job easier. Be a good example to the younger Scouts. Help them with projects and merit badges. Keep them enthusiastic about Scouting.

Attend Your Weekly Meetings

Your Scout group is probably the same as your priesthood quorum, which means that Scout activities give you the chance to develop skills and help to develop quorum unity. So be good about attending them.

Because of the complexities of life, it's not unusual for young men to occasionally become discouraged or depressed. Without your knowing it, many of your own friends might need a helping hand from time to time, a pat on the back, or even just a couple of hours away with "the guys" to recharge their batteries and energize their spirits.

That's one reason that Scout meetings and other quorum activities are so important. Even though *you* may not need any particular help, your presence might make the difference to someone else.

Live the Scout Oath and Law

A Scout is trustworthy, loyal, helpful . . . well, you know the rest of it. But do you really know what it all means? Find out! When you raise your arm to the square and recite the Scout Oath, you promise on your honor to do certain things, so you'd better know what you're promising.

A good way to start is by reading the Scout Oath and Law, then trying to understand exactly what they mean. Consider each word—look them up in a dictionary if you have to—and ask yourself, what does it really mean for *you* to be trustworthy? To whom do you show loyalty? How—and to whom—could you be more helpful?

When you recite the Scout Oath and Law, do it with conviction. Say them as if you're actually renewing a pledge, a pledge that you really mean to keep.

Scouting is a wonderful program, and I firmly believe it was inspired by our Heavenly Father. It changed my life and it can change yours too. The skills you learn will bless you on your mission, through college, and through all of your adult life.

Take advantage of them. Earn your Eagle (and don't wait until you're about to turn eighteen to do it). Choose a good Eagle project. Attend your meetings whenever you can. Live the Scout Oath and Law, and be sure to pass along your skills to the Scouts coming up behind you.

When you give it your best, Scouting will enrich your life. You'll have great adventures, learn valuable skills, and magnify your priesthood calling—all at the same time.

THE WORLD'S FASTEST
SCRIPTURE CHASER

Chapter Ten

Preparing for Your Mission

"Five."

Elder Chalks pedalled his bike up beside me. "What did you say?"

"Five," I repeated. "Tonight we're going to teach a family of five."

Elder Chalks laughed. "Five? Are you sure you haven't got your signals crossed?"

I shook my head. "I don't know," I said. "I've just got the number five in my head. And I've got a good feeling about it."

"Okay then. That's our goal . . . we don't go home tonight until we've taught a family of five."

I laughed. That's what I liked about my junior companion. He supported me in everything, no matter how goofy it seemed.

I had been on my mission in Japan for more than a year. And in all that time, I'd never taught a family of five. I'd rarely even *met* one. In Japan, families were rarely bigger than four.

Even so, I knew that tonight was going to be different. I could *feel* it. We were going to teach a family of five.

I didn't say anything to my companion, but I could almost see them: a father, mother, and three kids. I even thought I knew how old they were. There was a twelve-year-old girl, a ten-year-old girl, and an eight-year-old boy.

Everyone in the family was old enough to be baptized.

We pedalled to the neighborhood we had decided on and began knocking on doors. Things were slow at first, but about eight o'clock a friendly man invited us in. We introduced ourselves to him and his wife, then Elder Chalks began our discussion.

"*Chotto matte!*" Watanabe-san said suddenly. "Just a second. I'd like the kids to hear this too."

He called upstairs, and a moment later three children shyly trooped into the room: two ten-year-old twin girls and a seven- year-old boy.

I couldn't believe it. Elder Chalks grinned at me, then began telling the story of Joseph Smith.

I was transferred to another district before the Watanabe family was baptized, but meeting and teaching them was one of the highlights of my mission.

I loved my mission. I had such good companions and wonderful experiences that it changed my life forever. I became close to my Heavenly Father and developed a foundation of spirituality that's blessed my life ever since.

The Aaronic Priesthood is known as the preparatory priesthood. And one of the things it prepares you for is a mission. When you are honestly preparing to be an effective, enthusiastic missionary, you are magnifying your calling in the Aaronic Priesthood.

And it doesn't matter how old you are. Whether you're an assistant to the bishop in the priests quorum, a fifteen-year-old teacher, or the youngest deacon in the ward, it's not too early to begin preparing yourself.

In fact, the earlier you start, the more prepared you'll be. And the better you'll be able to serve your Heavenly Father.

So start now! Begin today and prepare to be the best missionary you can. Then, when the time comes, you'll be able to charge into your mission with the power of a hurricane. You'll turn your mission upside down, blessing the lives of others and laying up for yourself treasures in heaven.

Here's how to get started:

Read the Book of Mormon

You cannot underestimate the importance of studying the Book of Mormon in preparing for a mission and developing your testimony. Joseph Smith said that the Book of Mormon is the keystone of our religion and that you can become closer to your Heavenly Father by living its precepts than by any other book. And to receive a testimony of the restored gospel, you have to read the Book of Mormon. There's just no other way.

Besides, the Book of Mormon is the key to everything you'll teach, both in the mission field and in quorum meetings. The more you read it, the better you'll be able to teach.

Start a daily reading program. Read at least a chapter every day, but remember that your goal is not simply to finish the book. Ponder the Book of Mormon as you read it. Prayerfully seek the Spirit of the Lord and constantly ask yourself if you are truly reading the word of God. You will learn for yourself that the book is true.

Finally, test the promise in Moroni 10:3–5. Ask your Heavenly Father if the Book of Mormon is true. Have faith that your prayer will be answered.

President Ezra Taft Benson said that we need to constantly study the Book of Mormon, so once you've read it, don't stop! Read it again!

Or you could try a different approach. Choose a topic such as prayer, then search the Book of Mormon for references to prayer. Remember that the Book of Mormon was written for us— for you and for me—so search for ways to apply its message to your life.

You might also consider examining the lives of Book of Mormon teenagers. Read how Nephi handled problems with his brothers, for example. Discover how Alma and the sons of Mosiah prepared for their missions. Examine how Enos developed a testimony. You'll find that even though they lived thousands of years ago, young men in the Book of Mormon faced many of the same challenges you do. Their solutions might make sense in your own life.

President Benson said that the Lord needs missionaries who know and love the Book of Mormon. So read it! Ponder it! Study it and pray about it! As you do, the Book of Mormon will come to life. It will help you to become the motivated, testimony-filled missionary the Lord expects you to be.

Obtain Your Own Scriptures

When I was in ninth grade, I had a friend named Brice who was the world's fastest scripture chaser. He could track down scriptures faster than greased lightning.

One time I was leaning over his shoulder watching as his fingers flew through the pages. It was only a second before he found the right scripture.

"Contact!" he screamed. "Contact!"

He threw his hand straight in the air, smacking me in the eye. He hit me so hard he gave me a black eye. But he was so caught up in his scriptures that he didn't even feel it.

"Honest," he told me later. "I didn't even know you were hurt until I saw you rolling on the floor."

Anyway, I wanted to be as fast as he was. And so I asked him what his secret was.

"I know where all the scriptures are," he confided. "I don't have them memorized, but I know *exactly* where to look for them. One is in the back at the bottom of the page, and another one is in the front at the top."

As he talked, I realized that I basically used the same system. I didn't have all my scriptures memorized. But I had them marked. And I knew where to look for them.

Now, that might not be the best system in the world. But it worked. And when I went on my mission I knew my scriptures well enough that even when I didn't know the exact references, I could always find the scriptures I needed.

To be an effective missionary, you need to know the scriptures well. You need to be familiar enough with them that you can find the scriptures that you need.

Start by obtaining your own set. Then as you read them, mark those passages that strike your interest. Jot notes, thoughts, and explanations in the margins. Then, at times when you need a transfusion of spirituality, try thumbing through the pages, reading the scriptures you've marked. This way your scriptures will become personalized. They'll feel comfortable in your hands, and you'll get to know them as President Benson suggested.

Be Active in the Church

As a missionary, you'll ask people to read the Book of Mormon. You'll ask them to attend church. You'll ask them to live the Word of Wisdom and the law of chastity and to pay an honest tithe. You'll need to bear your testimony that the Lord expects his followers to do these things and that he will bless them when they do. In order to do that, you'll have to have a testimony of these things. If you wait until you become a missionary to gain one, that won't be easy.

While you hold the Aaronic Priesthood, live all the principles of the gospel so that you'll gain a strong testimony of them. Discover what happens when you really keep the Sabbath day holy.

Find out! Then your testimony will be packed with power and conviction.

Begin a Savings Program

Even if you don't have much money, start saving now for your mission. And if you have a part-time job, put aside a regular amount from every paycheck. This will help relieve the burden on your parents or anyone else who will be supporting you, and it will help to solidify your commitment to serve the Lord. It will prove your determination to serve a mission, and it will help to remind you that you're preparing to be a missionary.

Learn to Sew and Cook

When I was serving my mission in Japan, I was whipping up my favorite stew for dinner one evening when the other two elders in our district came in. Elder Durrant had a sullen look on his face.

"What's wrong?" my companion asked. "Bad day?"

"No." Elder Durrant dropped his books and slumped into a chair. He sighed. "It's just that it's Thursday again."

"So?"

Elder Durrant gestured toward me in the kitchen. "It's Thursday . . . and that means Elder Barker is making his disgusting stew for dinner."

I had never considered my stew disgusting before, but I realized that Elder Durrant was right. We each took turns cooking, and when my week came up I always made stew on Thursday. And spaghetti on Wednesday.

The truth was, I only had five or six recipes, and none of them would have won me any prizes. And according to Elder Durrant, my stew would have gotten me kicked out of a home economics class.

Chances are, you'll have to cook for your companions too. Don't wait until that day comes to learn to boil water!

A good way to start is by taking your turn cooking for your family. Make a list of your favorite meals, then have someone teach you to prepare them. Depending upon which part of the world you serve in, you might not be able to serve up everything you can at home, but at least you'll be able to keep things from sticking to the bottom of the pot.

In addition to cooking, it's smart to learn simple skills such as sewing on buttons and repairing a split seam in your slacks. Learn to do your own laundry too. Learn to iron and how to remove spots and stains from your clothing. You'll not only make your own life easier, but you'll bless your companions too.

Take Missionary Preparation Classes

One reason the Missionary Training Center is so effective is that returned missionaries will teach you to be an effective missionary. Most of your teachers will be fresh from the mission field, and they'll be able to teach you not only what works but also what doesn't. They'll be able to help you because they've been there.

You can get yourself off to a head start, though, by taking advantage of missionary prep classes in your ward and stake, if you have them. In them, you'll learn what the daily routine of a mission is like, and you'll get a head start on learning the discussions and missionary scriptures.

Then, when you are set apart and enter the MTC, you'll already have the momentum you need to rocket into your mission, making it one of the greatest experiences of your life.

The Lord expects you to serve a mission to bless the lives of other people and to give you an opportunity to grow and serve. Be excited about it! Look forward to it! Prepare yourself, and your mission will be one of the highlights of your life. Your experiences will bless you not only in this life but also in eternities to come.

HOW TO BUILD
A FIRE

Chapter Eleven

*The Blessings of Magnifying
Your Priesthood Calling*

Thirteen-year-old Logan Whitney blew into the tinder as gently as an anxious mother whispering to a newborn baby. A wisp of smoke curled away from the aspen shavings as the tiny flame crackled, sputtered, and died.

"Oh, man!" Logan sat back and brushed the mud off his knees. "I thought *sure* it was going to start this time."

Brandon Marshall peered over Logan's shoulder. "How many matches have we got left?"

Logan fished a wooden match from the pocket of his Scout shirt. "One. We're down to our last match. Any ideas?"

None of the four boys watching had any.

Logan shrugged. "Well, we've got one more match, one last chance. Let's make it good."

"Yeah," Brandon added. "Everybody go look for more wood. This one's got to be perfect!"

Logan kicked away the old fire lay as Brandon began looking for dry sticks. Two other boys began gathering piles of tinder. Someone else piled wood.

The five boys were part of a week-long Boy Scout leadership course. It was the last night of the course, and each patrol had been sent out to spend the night by themselves. Logan's patrol had followed a two-mile compass course deep into the woods and now, with darkness closing in, the boys were trying to get a fire going.

The only problem was that it had rained all day. The wood was wet. Every attempt the boys made to light their fire resulted in nothing more than half-hearted flames and a little smoke.

And now they were down to their last match.

The boys carefully reassembled their fire lay, then Logan held out the match.

"Well," he said, "here goes nothing."

"Wait!" Brandon said. He looked at each of his new friends. "Let's say a prayer."

Logan sat back and nodded. "Good idea." He looked around. "Any volunteers?"

A boy named James raised his hand. "I'll say it."

Without any embarrassment, the five boys knelt, took off their hats, and bowed their heads. James asked for help lighting the fire, then Logan struck the match.

"You should have seen it," Logan told me later. "That fire *flared* to life. And then you know what?" He grinned sheepishly. "All five of us cried."

Logan didn't need to feel shy about admitting that. I knew exactly what he was talking about. You see, you don't have to be a General Authority to work miracles. You don't have to hold the Melchizedek Priesthood. You don't even have to be president of your quorum.

Remember Joseph Smith? When he went into the woods to pray, he was suddenly overcome by the powers of darkness. But as he prayed harder, his Heavenly Father came to his aid. The Lord didn't abandon Joseph Smith. And when you need help, he won't abandon you either.

I used to work at a Boy Scout camp with a fifteen-year-old boy named Steve. We usually got our weekends off, but one time Steve had to return to camp early. He had to spend the night in his tent, alone, in the middle of the mountains.

"I was scared silly," he admitted. "Every time I started to get sleepy, a tree would creak and I'd imagine Bigfoot was sneaking up on me. Then I'd be wide awake again."

This went on for several hours, and just when Steve didn't think he could stand it any more, he remembered another time he'd been scared. His family had just moved into a new house, and it had scared him to sleep alone in his bedroom in the basement.

"But then during family home evening, my dad gave the house a priesthood blessing," Steve said. "In the blessing he said that as long as we lived the commandments and loved one another, our house would always be a place of peace and safety. And I was never scared again."

That experience gave Steve an idea. Of course, he didn't have the Melchizedek Priesthood, but he got up and knelt on his sleeping bag and asked his Heavenly Father to bless his tent and protect him in it.

"I know that sounds corny," Steve said. "But when I crawled back into my sleeping bag, it was like I was back home in my own bed. I went right to sleep."

Throughout this book we've talked about magnifying

your priesthood calling. Some young men might wonder, "Why should I?" And that's what I'd like to talk about now.

You need to know that your Heavenly Father loves you. He'll always love you whether you magnify your calling or not. But when you honestly strive to serve your Heavenly Father, when you do your best to magnify your priesthood calling, wonderful things happen. Let me list a few of them.

You Receive the Constant Companionship of the Holy Ghost

Having the Holy Ghost with you always means that you are entitled to revelations and visions that will guide you through school, work, and every other aspect of your life.

When I was in college, I constantly faced decisions about classes, work, and career choices. It could have been a time of misery, confusion, and frustration. But I was especially close to my Heavenly Father, and I felt the guiding influence of the Holy Ghost. There were times when I actually felt that the Lord had a hand upon my shoulder, guiding me along.

You face complex decisions in your life too. When you're worthy, the Holy Ghost will help you to make decisions not only of a spiritual nature but also relating to everything you do.

Remember that the Holy Ghost is also known as the Comforter. His calming influence will bless you in times of need, give you spiritual strength when you're weak or discouraged, and bless you with feelings of peace, joy, and happiness.

You Keep Yourself Worthy of Blessings When You Need Them

As a schoolteacher, I've often had students come to me at the end of the term, asking me to change their grades.

"I got a C last term," one boy told me. "And I've got to have a B."

I nodded. "So you want me to change your grade?"

"Yeah. If you will, I *promise* I'll do better next term."

Would any of your teachers go for that?

Probably not!

But suppose this boy came up to me a week or so before the end of the term. And suppose he said something like this: "I really need to get a B this term. And I think I've earned it. I've worked hard in class, I've turned all my assignments in on time, and I've done well on all my tests."

You can be certain that I'd take him a little more seriously!

Now, you can approach your Heavenly Father the same way. When you magnify your priesthood calling, you keep yourself worthy of receiving blessings when you need them. When you suddenly need the Lord's help, you don't need to bargain. Instead, you can approach the Lord with confidence, saying something like this: "I do my best to live the commandments. I keep myself clean and worthy of my priesthood. Please help me now."

When you approach your Heavenly Father this way, you can be confident that he will be listening.

You'll Become a Better Leader

As you advance through the Aaronic Priesthood, you'll be given many leadership opportunities in your quorum and in Scouting. In addition, you might occasionally be called to serve on youth committees in your ward, stake, or seminary programs. These positions will make you a better missionary and will prepare you for marriage, fatherhood, and leadership in the Melchizedek Priesthood.

When you receive the Aaronic Priesthood, you receive one of the greatest blessings a young man could ever have. You receive the power and authority to act in the name of your Father in Heaven.

But as we discussed earlier, it's not enough to simply have the priesthood. The Lord expects you to magnify your calling in it. He expects you to use it and make the most of it. He expects you to do your very best with it.

In the book of Abraham, the Lord said, "We will prove them herewith, to see if they will do all things whatsoever the Lord their God shall command them" (Abraham 3:25).

This is your chance to prove that you will do what the Lord has commanded you.

Be excited that you hold the priesthood. Use it, magnify your calling in it, make the most of it.

As you do, you will become one of the faithful servants to whom the Lord promised to give "all that my Father hath," which is eternal life in the kingdom of God.